The Reptilian Interludes
(and a child's prayer)

A long poem
by

ROSS TALARICO

a journey/retreat into the twenty-first century

BORDIGHERA PRESS

Library of Congress Control Number: 2008920523

Printed in the United States.

Published by
BORDIGHERA PRESS
John D. Calandra Italian American Institute
25 West 43rd Street, 17th Floor
New York, NY 10036

VIA FOLIOS 48
ISBN 1-884419-93-3

for my son Joseph, of course

*but also for all the sad scientists,
and all the bewildered poets.*

"I no longer dream of the stars"
— St. Augustine of Hippo, before 430 AD

"It would be an extravagant boldness for anyone to go about
and limit and confine the Divine power and wisdom
to some particular fantasia of his own."
— Pope Urban VIII, issuing warning to Galileo

"Man's capacity for neurosis would merely be the obverse
of his capacity for cultural development"
— Freud

"The body is just something to carry the brain around in"
— Thomas Edison

"Tools don't make us human, our love for them does"
— Lewis Mumford

"Science must inherit the moral imagination of man"
— Dr. Jacob Bronowski

theos ek mechanes
— The Greeks

TABLE OF CONTENTS

BOOK ONE
Existem Theorem: Journey and Dream

BOOK TWO
Ultima Ratio: Memoir, Discrete Structures, Prayer

AUTHOR'S NOTE

I'd like to thank the editors of Bordighera Press for publishing this book. When I asked them to consider it, they did something I could not get other editors to do (some of whom I've known for years): read it! Perhaps this is not the day and age when anyone, even our so-called literary merchants, can find the time to read such a long work, especially one that takes such an in-depth view of the species itself, one that tries to see our evolutionary connection to technology. Although I've had some successes with other books and the work I've done bringing together civil discourse and the poetic urgency of self-expression, this long poem seems to, for me at least, go a step further. I hope readers will be patient with it, and I hope my speculations on mankind and his/her journey will nurture a pondering of fundamental questions regarding who we are and the state of our humanity.

— R.T., June 2007

FOREWORD

Since the great Enlightenment split between the humanities and the sciences, the world of poetry has become increasingly impoverished, both in its vocabulary and in its grasp of the truths of nature (and of our nature). Ross Talarico has set himself to repair the breach in our sensibility and to recover the lost territories and languages of natural understanding.

Especially today, when creationists and evolutionists are at each other's throats, urged on by their theological handlers on both sides like dogs in a dogfight, and when our spiritual understanding of the world is at odds with our scientific understanding of it, a poetry that fully incorporates our evolutionary history is desperately needed. Though some of our best prose has recognized this need—Aldo Leopold, Loren Eiseley, Stephen Jay Gould, Douglas Hofstadter and Oliver Sacks come to mind—our poets have by and large neglected it. What Talarico evidently believes and demonstrates is that the world as understood through the scientific imagination is not less meaningful, less tragic, less spiritually and aesthetically beautiful, less humanly significant, than when viewed through the traditional literary lens.

— FREDERICK TURNER

BOOK ONE

~

EXISTEM THEOREM:
JOURNEY AND DREAM

PART ONE

I

I go into a book store,
ask for a book of matches,
am given them, free.

In the dark
I light one, and stare
for a long time after the flames goes out
into nothing

until I am nothing.
The eye finds its own glitter
of light;
in a cave in China
a spark flickers between two hearts
cramped and pumping
into a freak chest of single
mutant lizard.

Over the rich, chemical murk
of primitive seas
lightning sends a spark deep
into the beginnings
of order,

and there too the eye
is a witness, emerging from the water
to discover again

the arrangement of stars;
and it rises,

this eye, assuming
its evolutionary changes as simple
variations of light,
this common eye of ages,
one eye for all,
eye of man, of lemur,
of lizard . . .

It rises
through the hard black coal,
through the lush rot of vegetation,
through the lopsided, abandoned egg
of an oversized amphibian;

the eye finds its own glitter
of light,
and it rises
through the early misshapen bone
of spine,
through the glorious cellular transparency,
through the thin green leaves
that quiver with oxygen;

we lift our heads in a church,
and the eye rises,
through the buckling earth's crust,

through lava,
through simple rock;

it whirls with meteor
and creates the zigzag
of its pattern of vision,
its images unlinking, unlinking,
until the eye is pure light,
the very core of explosion,
the brilliant moment, however long,
before the complete destruction
of an earlier history;
the eye

about to explode into every fragment
of this poorly lit universe
filled with dream . . .

II

And so tonight my mind is
half-blank,
but still I know my way home.

I look up
knowing the stars I see
are no longer there.
That's no reason to disbelieve, I know,
anxiety is a human affair,
the watch on my wrist, illuminated,
keeps my pulse steady,
a spiritual synapse between blood
and neuron . . .

In bed, my breath in a slow fade
between sleep and death,
I recount, in an ancient prayer,
the three inborn fears
of this and every young primate:

I am falling, forever,
in the dark
which gets darker
and the snakes all around me
in a biblical garden
are beginning to utter my name . . .
and so I enter the dream

acceptingly, forgetting the concept
of acquaintance, disposing of
the brief interludes,
unsure of what comes clear
beside the salty waters of the eye.
My hair grows long
and flows in the current.
I drown once, twice,
and when I come up for the last time
I think of the stages
a man must go through to simply
worry about death.

This is the dream:
I dream I'm a man.
My hands, useless for a thousand years,
grasp a wrench.
The car lies disassembled, completely,
all around me.
The one wheel balanced perfectly
rolls off
toward an orbit of gleaming metals.
The instruments, strewn
over a wooded bench, spin recklessly.
Perched on the warm radiator,
a lizard.
I lift a wire to the hollow engine block
and a spark flies.
The windshield shatters.

I can find neither the problem
nor the key.
The warning light glows like a pineal eye
exposed to air.
I touch the wire to the antenna,
and a spark flies.
In the trunk I find the skeleton
of a man three and a half feet tall,
and when I touch the wire to it
there is light.
I listen to the radio.
One continuous piercing note
makes me sad to be away.
I touch my tongue
and a lesion occurs in the brain
and I sing along,
pure, instinctual.
I touch the wire to the lovely, bluish
puddle of gasoline,
and a spark flies . . .

III

A woman cries out,
her womb splitting, the blood-soaked flesh
surrounding the skull
as the body gives way painfully
to the oversized brain.

The scream carries
down a thousand corridors
until I arrive, half mad, in time
to push the child back
into the womb,
my hand disappearing deeper
into the moist, dark inner flesh;

I push further
and feel the skull shrink,
the skin turn leathery and cold,
and finally I feel
the round slippery eye
in the palm of my hand
and in the eerie silence of the earth revolving.
I start to weep . . .

My little boy gives me his hand.
He rises to his toes
as we walk
through the tall grass of the field.

My height
is a mystery to him.
The sun falls over us
so gently
we forget the blazing, eruptive source
and we are happier than men
have ever been.

I cannot tell him
what I don't know; his first words,
guttural and lyrical,
seem right.
He speaks with the animals
I can only domesticate
or fear.

I gaze out over the field
and with his small beautiful hands
he hangs on to my leg.
I inhale the unused oxygen
of his youth
as if to remember awakening myself
on a bed of blue algae
in the first blossoms of earth.

What can I tell you, Joseph?
There is never any peace.
Our memories are older than we are.
You are frightened by a snake.

I'm intrigued by physics.
We resemble one another,
but not exactly.
The wind is a lovely reminder of presence,
the flowers open
and the seeds surround us
with small and plentiful reasons for hope.
I wish it ended here;
we are natures' creatures, and you
are the most beautiful.
But there's something more, I know.
I start to tell you to stand straight,
but instead
I imagine some offspring
rising beyond height,
the last of our kind
pure energy
fulfilling the evolutionary dream
of extinction.
I love you son,
but all I can do for now is confess.

I am a killer.
Once I lifted a broken skull
and held it over me
in the chilly hollow
of its dark protection.
I painted the ceilings of caves.
I'm an artist too,

twenty thousand years crude,
painting what I hunt and love.
If I seem wise, it is
because I've turned fear into grace.
I keep you young, warm mammal,
brain constantly awakening,
so I can learn
why I am dying;
your lovely eyes gleam so . . .

IV

In Toledo,
In Rome,
In Vienna and so forth,
I am stunned
by the great cathedrals.

I rest my hand,
one small hand,
on the cold stone, cold metal,
and on the altar
the fire blazes . . .

I try to imagine the serenity
of creation,
the deep sparkle of a camera lens
fixed on the atom
at the long end of a stainless steel shaft.

Instead, I stand at the border,
afraid of a strange language,
holding onto a coin.
Once a silversmith etched my profile
on a bracelet;
whose wrist it circles now
I don't know.
There are many possibilities.
My imagination floats with the eerie

notes of a flute
as I make my way
through a subway tunnel in Paris
and discover
a train of blind schoolgirls.

I offer up the simplicity of speech
expecting in return the equal simplicity
of music and prayer.
But my insistence on understanding
is the silence we behold,
is the dignity we live by,
is the struggle to accept what we are
and what we are not.

A deaf mute
edges his way forward
until he sees the choir . . .

PART TWO

I

An eye floats on the rectangular waters
of a rear-view mirror.
Behind me the world fades and blurs
until speed is the perfect abstraction
of being.
I close my eyes,
and the eye in reflection
fills with light.

Five hours on this lousy road.
According to the phrase
spread over the back of a 2-ton semi
Wilkes Barre, Pa is the place
where the great roads meet.
I guess we all believe in heaven,
no matter what we're hauling.
A trooper passes by, glances over,
speaks into his transmitter
and speeds off
in pursuit of his magical voice.

I have my own laws to obey.
Every year I try to
make it back
to the place I was born.
But unlike the young hunter
who twenty years ago

brought home
a stray cat and the music
of sea shells,

now my hands are empty;
for a moment I even
let go of the wheel.
Just east of Moline the radio
goes dead.

So I dream,
seventy miles an hour,
thirty-two hundred r.p.m's,
the accelerating, unmeasurable blink
of the eye
as I come to the binocular understanding
that we abandon the
childhood of our species however we attempt
to return, for speed,
for the calculated gamble of evolutionary leaps,
this foot strangely pressed to the floorboard . . .

And why home;
why do we return at all?

What or whose
origin do we seek?
I try to answer plainly,
citing the countryside like a primitive farmer

trying desperately to love
the terrifying requirement of a fixed abode.
But there is no reason to ritual,
only a vague, incessant faith
in beginnings.
My chant as I approach the puny holy land
of my upstate New York home
is a popular song
sung by a confessed orphan who's won
the silly consumer hearts
of an America bent on the penance
of an easy beat as recognizable
as a salesman's cologne.

Outside, a hitchhiker holds out
his thumb,
and as I pass his monotonous wait
transforms the gesture
into the measurement of an artist
contemplating his subject.
I light a cigarette,
take the earth into my lungs
and breathe out clouds to cover

the world I leave behind,
the stranger on his chancy romantic journey
under the iron ore skies
beginning to spark
in Ohio.

II

In October
we don the masks of beasts
and roam
through the sugary homes
and find in the presence of strangers a compliance
to this awkward drama of the past.

The colorful leaves
fall
and the seventy shades of red and yellow
fall through
the remote, unchanging season
in the dark cavity of the chest.
At night
the bonfires blaze up
and in the light of the burning leaves
we forget, once again, that bond
between anticipation and death,
autumn's vague aesthetic forming in our minds.

What finally burns pure
is our love
for leaves burning, for the moment
at the smokey verge of disappearance,
for the universe as we know it,
a mild and clear October night
filled with creatures made believable
by our ancient memory.

Our fear too goes up in smoke
as we gaze out, strangely peaceful
in the blind harmony of all
living things,
toward the stars we know
have moved on,
and in that brief interlude
the lizard too removes its costume
and basks in the refracted starlight
that falls inward
from the eye . . .

Somewhere deep, deeper
In the forest
the beast once more has fallen
in love, and stalks
the girl who tiptoes at the edge
of his huge, serene shadow.
He is sorry for the antelopes
held too tightly, for the weight
of tears that have shattered mirrors,
and he knows the myth
of his becoming a man, beautiful and vain,
and he knows there must be
a passion more calm than his,
more lasting . . .

My mask glued to my face
I begin to panic
as I see the arm of the young girl,

who may be anyone tonight,
pass like a wand over her departure.
The bare vagrant limbs
of a tree
have fallen across my shoulders,
and I steady myself,
the last tonight of the fully alive.
The flame in the pumpkin flickers,
but it too grows strong
and in the morning light
nothing has changed.

III

A while back,
according to some recent calendar
or another,
I stood between the headless monuments
of gasoline pumps
and breathed the flammable air
around me.

Before the junking of the Studebaker
I raced the engine,
listened to the song of the oil pump,
two hundred black gloves
stroking the iron block.

I spun the tires,
let them burn and scream their way
into an oblivion too distant
for their 50 or 60 thousand miles
of wear.

And in one final bearing-busting rev,
to the inevitable tow,
the tailpipe coughed up the last
dark echoes of voices . . .

I remember
how worn out the regional celebrity
appeared

in his last visit
to the revolving sports car display
at the yearly auto show.
I was young, dreaming of
speed and chrome,
never considering the time it takes
to learn
that love for machines
equals the shame we feel
for our inadequacies.

Even in our poorest attempt
to transfer energy
we stumble back
to the strange cuddle of sleep
as if to anticipate
the first light.
But it's only a brief nap
between eras,
and once again I drive the night road,
like a man obsessed with the night road,
knowing this car is obsolescent,
as is everything in the world
including the only species
that writes poetry . . .
wondering what dies first,
man or his inventions,

the idle energy of hope
or the brilliant idea upon impact?

IV

Employing the electro-magnetic spectrum
I send a love-note
to the stars,
post-romantic radio freak
that I am . . .

In older days
across the immaculate blackboard
I let my chalk finger screech
and scribble
The word for *word.*
Writing, or course, is an invitation
to forget,
our memories a clutter
of referential data, including the whereabouts of
the portable guide to instinctual behavior.
The illiterate, during a bawdy
impersonation of limbic calls and cries,
began singing, without reason
and melodiously,
the numbers of his social security card.
That night,
during the lull of an oil embargo,
staring at the gleaming tombstone
of a cash register,
I tried to write my first poem:

Of course I was alone,
without shelter,
discovering myself part by part
with each limb, each bud, each
blade of grass,
each stone which sent its weight
through thigh, calf, imperfect toes
into the earth
which I rhymed, naturally, with birth.
I lost myself in the abstracts
of desires, obsessed with an image
of a spotlight in the wilds
as I followed my dog deeper
into the unexplored woods,
tracking the scent of lost child,
escaped convict, until I found myself

without laughter though delighted
at the joke of any knowledge of paths.

On the clock somewhere
above me
each lost moment became
a mechanical lapse into which
I crammed the unbelievable man-hours
allotted me . . .
I saw my dog begin digging
and so I began digging too.

My fingers were the impatient roots
of a consciousness bent
on an interlocking bond between man
and earth.
My dog found a bone
and when he chewed it was the bone
of my hand he was chewing.
But I kept on digging,
this crude burial wrought with love.
I dug and uncovered
skull and bowl, fossil and tool.
I found the huge backbone
of something I can't image,
and evidence of fire,
and deep into the earth I felt
a strange thick sea
until my hands were oil and my body oil
and I rose gloriously
at the touch of a steel drill
and burst into a black fountain on earth
and filled the pumps before me
with the blood of the past
and waited for the spark
that comes form the man the inventor,
the imitator,
man the worshipper of the fiery star . . .

Just before closing
I cleaned, meticulously, the tools

which I own free and clear.
I threw away the poem,
understanding my two week vacation
in the Adirondacks each year
was no more than a diversion
to allow a man
a gradual separation from the lovely history
of his nature.
I checked the locks on the station door
and for a moment
expected to see my hand the skeleton
I had written of;
I locked myself out and drove off,
disobeying the speed limit
but never fast enough
to outrun my headlights as I squinted forth
through the night.

PART THREE

I

Last night
on the eve of my mother's funeral
I arrived at home.
Coming over the hill
I saw the lights of the city
sparkle forth like the highlighted points
of a massive diamond.
I laid claim to the false document
of memory,
until my childhood too glittered once more,
care free
and vaguely symptomatic.

A few snowflakes
disappeared into the dark shiny pavement,
and the first of
many chills to come shot through me.
The warm air of the car heater
blew over me;
I thanked god for the effect
of environments, for the temperature range
of blood, for the umbilical cord
filled with that blood,
severed now, and tied in a bow
over my mother's body.

In the backyard I
come across

the stump of the old cherry tree,
its white blossoms still aburst
in the silk boxes
filled with photographs
in the damp fruit cellar where I
first kissed the cold cheek
of a girl.
The rose bushes are still thick,
the stems covered
with thorns; I touch them
again, remembering how I confused
blood and rose,
pain and infatuation, as I ran
all the way to a house that was empty, always empty,
and stinking of perfume.

And still in the yard
rusted, the cold metal cracked
and rotting, almost letting go,
the glider swing.
I reach up and touch the place
where the weld was made,
where the steel melted under the
fierce flame,
where metal, fire and the air we breathe
forged together
with a strength I
trust and feel pass through me,
another chill,

as I sit on the swing
on this cold autumn day, the sun
gleaming off the buffed weld
which holds like a miracle
as the glider squeaks and I swing higher,
higher, knowing I must contact
the garbage service
to get rid of this hulk,
and swinging higher
knowing the weld will hold
longer than I can hold the spirit
of a summer afternoon
with my mother in full bloom . . .

II

I try to tell the doctor
she is not dead.

He picks up her wrist,
gingerly, as if it were a first date.
He places his ear to her breasts.

He lifts her eyelids
and shudders at the two blank worlds
reflecting his image,
I tell him she is not dead.

He holds a mirror to her lips
and waits for a small
quivering fog.

The glass was never so clear.
But no, no, she is not dead.

See if she can dance I say.
But he doesn't know how.

Tell her that you love her,
but he's neither a lover
nor a liar.
Tell her the old joke; but
even I have forgotten it.
I try to tell him she is not dead.

Pound on her chest,
threaten her with a knife;
tell her she is not dead
and a bad storm is coming . . .
But he's neither liar
nor lover,
and finally he dangles the power cell
before her, attaches the wires,
removes the pacemaker from the vat
of liquid that erases
every trace of human susceptibility,
and in a last ditch hypnotic stare
he tells all of us
we are not dead . . .

Again, as I look in the mythical past
when we all survived,
an electric jolt racks the asynchronous heart
back into its intrinsic rythmicity.
3000 volts to come back from the dead,
a burn on the chest
a tattoo of loves too distant
to understand.
One woman, equipped with
two implanted pace makers, one for heart
one for liver,
claims now a new rapport, a feeling,
for things mechanical.
In a car she is the engine;
watching the clock, she
feels herself tick.

I try to tell the doctor she is not dead.

The metallic skull of a
firstborn child
gleams in the moonlight birth
in a canyon filled with the static echoes
of a short-wave radio.
Amazed at the adjustments of
human brain cells,
another expendable being dreams
of living forever.

There are many possibilities.
In a hundred test tubes stored
in a warm vault
the whim of science reproduces itself.
I try to think
what I'll contribute to the future:
my love for lilacs,
the correct way to pivot on second base,
the polished tools in my trunk?

Somewhere a dying star explodes,
its charged particles
falling like ashes through the dark
ancient sky of the sleep
that overtakes us.

Sometimes we die off, whole species;
sometimes we sleep through the night.

To create we must dream;
to dream we must abandon certainty.

I lift the phone,
turn my voice into the true speech
of electricity,
and announce, finally, my mother's death.
I open the desk drawer
and rummage through the contents:
a pen out of ink,
an unused pocket calculator,
a horoscope torn out of a book,
a letter written in a language
I can't identify.
From the top of the desk
I pick up her old companion,
the caged lizard.
I take it to the backyard
and set it free in the grass.
For a few minutes
neither of us move . . .

III

On the morning
of her funeral, long after
my son's eyes open
my eyes remain closed.
What I accept in dream
is the rich, vital preoccupation
with presence.

Sometimes, in the night, an eyelid rises
for no reason,
the light drifting out, as the Greeks and Romans
originally, mistakenly and gloriously claimed,
and everything becomes the eerie focus
of human awareness,
perspective nothing but a simple-minded guess
at the proximity
of something a man runs endlessly towards.

A reptilian hiss commands silence,
a laser lights up
the tunnel that does not end.
I dream in order to awaken,
to find myself balanced
between incomplete histories and
unimaginable futures.
What I accept in a dream
is the surprise of awakening,

the senses grasped like the handle
of a gun under the pillow,
the sight of a statue of the virgin
on the nightstand next to the bed,
her acceptance, and mine, of the miracle
of a routine birth,
and the unexpected love of a child
which is all we can
hope for, or hope to be.

What I accept in dream is the dreamer.

⮑

. . . I begin by
not moving at all.

Each moment breaks down
into the ignorant beats of the heart.
with every breath I give up
the secret of the wind
flutters before me.
My shoulders are two mounds of dust
beginning to petrify.

My arms tear themselves
from their one embrace, until I
move forward, my body
filling the gaps in the wind,

my fingers, in some intrinsic grasp,
taking root in the air.

Far off, a shadow moves
toward its completion; one step
after another
takes me into and out of
my past . . .
For a while I follow
any path, alongside a river
that winds to struggle free
from the earth it gives life to.
At the faintest howl
the eyelids flinch, in both memory
and anticipation.
Small branches break
as I clear my way through,
and in my lungs
the lovelier branches of veins begin breaking
as I try to breathe
for everything around me.

Under the path I wear
I hear the lullaby of the stream,
cold blue vein of earth;
at the waterhole
my hands lift the burden
of my own thirst.
I take a sip of water,

resolving the crisis:
I shall live . . .

Across the prairies
I shall live
with the evenness of temperament,
allowing the sky
its vast, secret wish,
lying flat with the earth
and hearing the faint pulse
of the root.
I am the instrument through which
everything sings.
I rise, I follow,
I bury the dead in the tell-tale graves
of my footprints.

Under a rock
where the fire smolders
I examine the crude utensils
I shall live with
and without
in the haste of my departures.
Two ponds appear and
disappear

as I trudge forward, through illusion,
through hunger too great
for this world alone;

The first dead meat rots
in the evolving stomach.
The rank breath becomes speech,
my first request:
that someone is listening . . .

And what do you hear,
companion, counterpart, supposed singular
object of love?
I clear my throat, cough,
and you see danger.
Between us the germ spreads.
We grow strong, together,
developing the immunity of
each other's presence.
Even your instinctual flight
is nothing more
than a mating dance;
and I catch you, fight you,
enter you, and sometime, years after
you give birth and discover
the unruly epic of human care,
I begin to love you . . .

Now, neither of us know
what was expected of us.

The last time I put my head down
and listened

I felt the dry earth cracking
against the smooth curve
of my ear,
and there, far above the volcanic sea
bubbling in the wide open
hearts of the dead,
there, I was able to recall
what I could no longer see,
the stream that once
kept me alive;

and I sucked in the red dust

and by memory alone
I repeated the vow,
I shall live, and that was the echo
in the telescope's tunnel,
that was the plea
of the heretic scientist

grown dizzy from predictable,
sensible revolutions.
I shall live
was the absent-minded poet's translation
of the ape's brotherly grunt
as he jumped from the bridge
and in that instant
sung the only phrase he had ever
come to understand.

And, in 1874 to be exact,
a man named Tyndall
discovered that
the living and the dead were composed
of the same matter.
I study the contour
of hand, of rock,
of hip, of compositional metal,
of buttock, of plastic,
professing my smooth love
and not knowing
where I become the thing
I adore.

A heart thumps in the center
of a missile,
and when I stir, the hypnotic countdown
brings me back
to sleep's effortless journey
from reptile to star.
There I am, rubbing my eyes
at the edge of a city
in the year 2000, the book of knowledge
under my arm
and still unable to utter
one acceptable truth.

And yet I know who I am.
I wait patiently
for an interstellar message

or simply
a tap on the shoulder.
Across the blackboard
in an abandoned schoolhouse
the demolition man writes
I shall live . . .
All those years of learning
how to survive,

all those poems, religions and tears;
and in a cellar, his initials etched in
the cold stone foundation,
a boy barely old enough
to understand calculus
attaches three wires to a human heart
kept in a sterile jar.
It is Christmas,
and though this is just a kit
and no miracle,
it is a gift that will occupy him.

IV

In a secret military training ground
someone attaches, literally,
a mounted gun
to a human eye:
aim, focus, invariably kill.

Is this a dream?

No, it is the year 2000.

Someone lifts an eyebrow,
the slightest gesture tapped and
channeled electrically,
activating an automotive braking system
and cutting reaction time
more than 50%;
a child walks across the road, safely.

Is this a dream?

The amputee simply thinks about
raising his plastic arms,
and his arms rise,
the embrace complete . . .

It is the year 2000.

A few months after birth
the brains of babies
are implanted with electrodes.
This is an experiment, no doubt,
and not meant
to substitute pleasure for will.

In the midst of certain death
a man smiles,
the dust of uncontained energy
settling within him
like a beautiful grey drift
under the vast solar wind . . .

I don't know how long
I slept,

or if my mother became a saint,
or if a saint is simply an odd variation
of man made
in his creator's image;
I don't know how long it was,
but I kept on dreaming . . .
When the roads straightened out
and the smoke cleared,
and the charged particles lit
the enchanted sky,

I still walked alone
and before me lay
the spontaneous pale yellows blossoming
over the huge, gentle slopes
of gravitational fields,
and in the distance, intermittent
light and sound,
one enormous computer in a state of bliss.
I felt the constant rush
of chemical molecules
spilling into my blood, the small
explosions of protein,
the cheap, insistent thrill
of implanted sensors
as I took in the world around me
by mere thought alone
and desires so basic I sent out
the common song of a man
through the electric impulses
of my newly strengthened
vocal cords.

Above me, the sun
poured forth its promise, the skin
converting the light
directly into energy, my journey
effortless now, the flesh
turning a light green, soft
and lovely,

the word *nature* its prayerful stimulant
programmed with synthetic messages
into the portable cell.

I felt the first smooth
mendings of mouth
and nose, as they closed toward
the inevitable seal

and the thinning air filled
with the glowing, winged creatures
of radiation
in a singular migration
to space, to spirit.

Tired, bored,
I hooked my conductor appendage
to a wild seed terminal,
lay back,
and through me
all the rage, love, and fidelity
transmitted itself
in one continuous sexual wave
toward the sky still blue with hope;
at once, my wishes
mere realities,
I was the ecstatic transducer,
both instrument and message
of this world

on the shaky verge of discovery
and obsolescence . . .

On the near horizon,
in a nuclear pond, trying to see
the image I've become,
man in man's image
machine in God's name,
the eye floats
as if in a solitary drift
apart from the struggle between
lightness and dark.
And when I look into it
I am dazed by the hypnotic glow,
dazed by the swirling tear
that forms
in the haunting depths
of the witness's eye,

my eye,
someone's eye
floating in the nuclear pond
where our unconsciousness
remains sunken
in the soggy, cell-struck bottom,
there among the treasures
waiting for the spark,
the old lightning,
the radioactive hook and line,

waiting for my strength
as I heave myself backwards
in some melancholy lapse
into an earlier evolution,
the one-sided battle
between man and fish, land
and water
lung and gill,
this lapse, a fluke memory,
and all the while
the image rises to the surface
of the floating eye,
cybernetic man stupidly casting a line
without hunger or need . . .

On the crisp, volatile edge
a reptile suns itself,
and blinks twice at the slightest stir
of the humming air.
. . . I hold my son's head
close to my heart
as he sobs at the sight
of his grandmother's casket.

In his quick glance
into the coffin
he mistakes

the rosary around her hands
for a black rope
and he shudders,

as I do,
my labored breath the involuntary evidence
of the life I whisper soothingly
into my son's tender ear.

I want to say
that the dream is not over,
that I, that we
have just awakened from it
for a while.
Instead I say *she is*

at rest now, at peace.
The priest celebrates
the miracle of the consecration
of the Host,

and escaping in a dark
immortal glow
upward, outward,
each plucked soul emits
a note of higher pitch, higher frequency,
until the priest
in the midst of his off key chant
feels the silent chill of the certainty

of his own unexplained death,
and warms his hands over the flame
on the altar.

Outside, in the cold air,
I tug my wool collar closer
around my bare neck,
and my boy does the same.
Above, a satellite
picks up the lukewarm waves
emitting from the two small places
we occupy in this world.
I shrug my shoulders,
as if a simple gesture repeated
time and time again.
can become an instinct, the
urge to fly:
the good sense to walk away . . .

We have a long walk, Joseph,
there is an incomprehensible quickening of pace.
The simple discoveries made
along the way
are hidden now in the lovely gleam
of a sad boy's eyes . . .

Be patient.
We are waiting to be someone's past.

BOOK TWO

∽

Ultima Ratio:
Memoir, Discreet Structures, Prayer

PART ONE

I

In Spring
the first buds burst defyingly
on the beautiful dying oaks.

The electric organ
has been unplugged for more than
two weeks now,
and I'm glad.
I toss the small leather ball
high into the air
and my son has a danceful way
of being under it
when it falls.
I give him the advice
of a 17th century philosopher,
to see the world as it is;
and he follows the spin of the sphere,
the windy slant
of its graceful descent, and determines
the speed of a falling object
seeking its proper place in the world,
his rich, dark, leather glove.

The slow curve I pitch to him
hangs in the air,
and I can't explain
the sudden misdirection, or the force with which

any two particles in the universe
attract each other.
He simply swings the bat, and connects.
The blackened skulls rise
through the measurable, layered earth,
the birds lower their cries
and everything directs itself
toward the joyous surface
where, for a moment,
the baseball suspended between our
precise and starry gazes,
we seek and find our proper place
in the world ...

The last chunk of ice
sends out a sparkling beam
of reflected light
from the distant center of the lake.
Snow tires thaw
in the dark corners of cellars.

The new paint glistens
under the short repetitive strokes
of the dreamy handyman.
The schoolteacher touches the arm
of the slender, blond co-ed
who leaves the book open now,
for days at a time,
at the same, half-read page.

A cluster of pheasant
fly up noisily
and circle ritually the new
and empty space,
the gunshot echoing through valley, ear
and memory . . .

The bride's family poses for the portrait.

A simple name turns a head;
or is it the voice
with which it is spoken?

II

The image settles in the mirror;
how long can a man stand there
examining
his impeccable presence.
It took so long to find the proper place,
the proper light.
His eyes gaze deep
into the simple, simpler truth
of what he sees.
How long can a man stand there
examining
his impeccable presence
in such a fragile place
which he sought and found properly
in this world . . .

I take a long look.

The lines on my face are
the deep ruts
left by my ancestors
in their hasty mappings of earth.
The grease stains on my hands
don't wash off anymore.
But my age seems fixed,
the bone turned jewel
as so many poets have claimed.

The Reptilian Interludes

The heart finds its strongest,
most lyrical rhythm;
the eye surrounds the human aesthetic
and it holds it
at the center of all vision
until inside the storm
of our evolving brain
an ideal is locked in the black hole
of memory,
and it consumes us day by day
until we are not ourselves anymore.
There is a moment, a hundred years or more,
or however long,
when each species discovers
its proper place
in the unaccountable, barely recorded
history of this world;
and it passes, unknowingly, with time.

I look at myself,
happy now
with my unextravegant good looks.
There's a woman waiting for me,
and I will seek my place beside her.
In the miraculous contentment
that comes with knowing
that there is no knowing
it is not difficult to understand
the simple love I have

for this clean white shirt,
or this finger-tip of cologne,
for the shine of this shoe
which may seek this print
in cement
as the foot, more easily, seeks its
in the illusive choreography of dust.

III

At dawn
I glance around this house crammed
with the artifacts
of a life spent arranging
a decorative order.
Upon the red corduroy overstuffed couch,
the impression of last night's vigil;
the brass lamp is a fixation
between antiquity and perpetual light.
The bookcases are neatly stacked
with the obituaries
of a thousand former identities.
The carpet, if I stare
at its oriental design, confuses me.

This is the life we have chosen,
external, well-mannered,
half slave half God
to some casual sequence of numbers,
the cost of a vase,
those repetitious chants
with which we keep count of ourselves,
of our efforts,
of the romantic lotteries
and the hundred near misses
and the consistency of hope.

I packed a carton of junk:
an old music box filled with dust,
a chipped crystal ashtray,
a faded photograph of an ancestor's farm,
a tarnished sax without a mouthpiece.
In the pawn shop,
through the narrow, cluttered aisles,
the frightened young burglar
prays for guidance
and forgiveness,
the alarm blaring in a nearby precinct,
the policemen
already drawing their guns . . .

What can we hope for
with our accidental habits, our
mediocre aim?
Spontaneously, we are criminals
or artists.
In some hankering for law
we become, just as quickly, victims,
the first casualties, the only respectable
proof of our worth.
In spirit, we are the blessed meek;

romantically, we cling like seeds
to the bloody paw
of something almost dead;
and realistically . . . realistically,

between the flowering eulogy, between the
violet petalled banner
that casts waving shadows across the white stone,
between the beautiful austere tomb
and the strange approximate survey of the vast, holy
flat earth beyond
a man walks a lifetime or more
back and forth
over the rare, intricate, hand-made carpet,
the blood soaked ground
upon which
we sleep and wake and place our lips
and kiss . . .

A car mechanic is almost
obsolete;
at the very least it's hard
to make a living.
The spark never dies now,
the metal never wears.
If an object attains the proper speed
there is no need for maintenance.

My wrenches gleam on the rack.

In my spare time,
learning to read, comprehend, and calculate
in one graceful, instinctive motion,
I try to determine the potential efficiency

of forty two hundred
multiple warhead missiles on any
given day.
By my figures, my guess,
a neuron bomb would leave
every self-sufficient, energy transferring computer
completely intact.
I drift, magnetic dust through the universe,
until I try once more
my primitive hand at a poem,
strange amateur that I am;

but how can I say
the bomb seeks its place
in the air as the center of light
and in the earth
as the lid to darkness and prayer . . .

IV

On the white sheet,
on the cool flesh of strangers,
on the crumbling foundation
of incomprehensible mortgages,
we sleep and wake and place our lips
and kiss ...

Tragedy is nothing more
then a declarative sentence graced
with a question mark.
At age three, my son accidentally shot and killed
his mother, my wife.
I write out, without punctuation,
purely,
as if listing for no reason a dream,
the words
life must go on

A woman's voice
drifts out of the phone.
Her questions are the lovely curves
of breasts, of buttocks, shoulder
and knee.
In the background the music
drives me,
breath, hands, voices
alive on the instruments, each amplified

and recorded
until I am surrounded by electricity
and desire.
Even my son records his voice
on the magnetic echo of tape.

There is a school of thought,
call it the toolmaker's,
which claims, as far back as the
12th or 13th century,

that the flowing rhythm of the ivory Virgin
was due merely
to the curve of the elephant's tusk.
The artist shrugs his shoulders
and walks away
from the thing he loves.
All men imagine themselves
on crusade, returning, lost,
craftsmen spreading the news;
and when a woman gives birth
a man compensates for his absence
with a belief in miracle.

The fact is
a man imagines his absence
the way a woman conceives
a multiple of presence.
In the last war-cry

a man hears himself whispering
the sorrowful utterance
of his obsessive creative cycle,
the toolmaker's paradox:
the explosion and the enlightenment.
The miracle
is his regret.
Everything else is an evolutionary
sense of duty . . .

Mold forms
on the concrete folds at
the feet of St. Modeste
on the northern portal.
On the ceiling of the Palazzo Barberini
and in the constant light of our eyes
the figures fade
into some wild guess of human strategy,
the spirited touch
of finger upon thigh barely a passion,
no longer a choreography
but merely the brief and inconsolable whim
of a chance intimacy . . .
Two satellites, thousand of years old,
pass inches apart
adrift in calculated, starry orbit.
A monitor blinks like a perfect eyelid.
Someone calls me a lover.

I cling to the flesh replica
of my own foolish ideal:
life must go on . . .
On the cool flesh of strangers,
on the crumbling foundation
of incomprehensible mortgages
we sleep and wake and place our lips
and kiss . . .

In another room,
what world?
my son screams at the nightmare
of blood;
once more he has killed his mother,
and the dreamsmoke from the gun barrel
rises
like billowing signals
at the edge of enormous cliffs
jutting out over the calm blue light
of the universe . . .

PART TWO

I

Cupped in my palm,
the tiny, rare firebird;
the small flame
lights up the underside
of my hand
as I back away
from the glowing air.

It is a flickering warmth
I associate
with spirit; and though
I imagine the leaves on fire,
the sky ablaze with light
and melody,
I look away from the glowing air.

You, Joseph, are captivated
by the momentary captivation
of this small creature
whose bones
could be crushed by
mere anger alone.

You stare, touch,
its light flickering in your eyes.
The wings flap
against my palm

and you look at me
not knowing what to expect
nor the meaning of freedom.

What are our options,
son,
the rare firebird in our grasp?
I lift my hand
and there is joy, then sadness
as all things return
to their natural state, the firebird,
the sky,
you and I, captors and liberators,
lovingly
to the earthly retreat from the glowing air.

. . . I try to decide
whether the manual switches
are necessary.

The voltage pulse
passes from the brain through hand
to electronic logic circuits
which determine
the storage for capacity
and the quantity of binary digits
necessary.

Necessary?

Nevertheless I discover
the obvious: the narrower the pulse
the faster the computer.

I allow for additional circuits
to process
the updated information
sent form the Central Processing Unit,
but by this time,
the machine art begun,
this introduction to discreet structures,
the inevitable anti-poem,
I accept the knowledge of my input
as irrelevant subjectivity
and leave out
whole decades at whim,
choosing haphazardly
the measurable time-space shapes
of emotions
that signal the brain potentials
of cybernetic intelligence.

I know,
I'm just learning.
As of now I'm technically incompetent.
This is just a hobby.
I close my eyes.
As a boy, lost
in the thick wood I stumbled

upon a meadow, bewildered
by the flora exotica.
Still,
hurtling through the dark
of my eyelids,
the fragmented color bombards me,
gold and purple,
Chrysanthemum and Hyacinth,
the simplest wish
spilling over under the stark rainbow of Iris,

the most innocent curiosity
an explosion of Sunflower.

Inside my chest I
bleed openly, lovingly, with the Rose . . .

I connect the multigraph
of four verticals,
amazed once more at the symmetry
of my own design,
and later
at the state of oscillation
in which we unite,
divide,
and sub-divide.

Eulerian cycle,
Hamoltonian path,

Lilium, Seersucker, Dahlia.
I close, I close
my eyes, as all eyes must close
on the sadness of memory . . .
To be human, I start to read,
absent-mindedly,
into the processor, but the gates
and inverters signal crazily
in the circuit module
and instead I type out the code
for unification
and transduction.

I fell asleep in that meadow,
and never woke up.
I don't think there is
any measurable time-space shape for love,
only this hypnotic desire
to join with the object of *perpetual* love,
that mystery we swear by.
Somewhere along
the sequential transmission of circuitry
my uncertainty records itself.
Between my finger
and the last manual switch
the spirit passes.

II

Trying to understand
the time-lag factor, master
and slave
separated by so many miles
even signals traveling
the speed of light pose a problem
of coordination . . .

And later, in some
simpler contemplation, trying to
understand the lyrics
of a poet dying happily
on the West Coast,
I put the books
back on the shelf, depression
turning into
the partially-memorized, empty-handedness
of the universal;
I decide

to adjust this language we have
almost sung,
and remove the words that remind us
how close we came
to being ourselves.
For instance:
Beauty . . . in each of us, of course,

originally synonymous with the eye itself,
something to behold; a series of notes
and the echoes of mirrors;
powder on the face of the corpse.
Beauty, the word; there is no need for it.

Truth. How strong our denial,
how elegant the quick logic
of a good guess now
and then.
Salt water, gravity,
the revolution of one body
around a mind.
The approximate size of a bird's heart.
A fire blazes
on an icy acre of space,
and in my eyes
two portraits, icicle and flame,
hang in some abandoned gallery
of a final human retrospective.
We still insist
the plot must be unified;
ignorant of history, ashamed
at the blind nostalgia of poetry,
I look for truth
but find only knowledge.
Inevitably I employ
the *deux ex machina*; unexpectedly I suffer
a change of fortunes.

A single word on a page
is out of context.
Truth, I take out truth.

Dark must go, too poetic.
I remove dark from the language.

Oblivion, and its counterpart,
Essence . . . it saddens me to say them,
saddens me more to consider
their loss.

Teresa, the word, gone blank
on the hidden document.

Sentimentality,
and *sentiment* as well.

Soul, I remove it
with the delicacy of a surgeon;
it disappears easily, leaving no space,
no scar.

Salvation, reason, luck, jet-lag,
I remove them all.

Also, *love,*
the dark edge
of light's expanding beam;

Light, so permanently fixed as word,
as wonder,
must remain, and with it
love disappears.

Finally, I rid myself of *suddenly;*
not because it's too
convenient a transition,
as I was told early on,
but because nothing happens suddenly,
nothing. *Suddenly,* gone.

. . . The book of dead language
grows heavy with time.
The white-haired arthritic,
under the filtered light, turns slowly
the crisp pages.
It is a beautiful room,
the sheer gathered curtains
blow lightly
in the last fading chorus
of an aimless wind.
The porcelain bowl, so utterly empty,
glistens in the truest of
still lifes.

On the bare wall, a portrait
breaks into light and dust,
the essence of impressionistic impulse,

the art of oblivion,
until the woman is unrecognizable,
the poem of her name forgotten.
He is the last of us,
his labored breath a painful echo
of the firstborn's sweet song.

In a window's endless transparency
the dark horizon
settles in the vacancy of his eyes;
He is the sole occupant.
And when he lay his head
onto his arms
he becomes the light of the eye arisen
until we see him, clearly,
suddenly gone.

III

On a warm spring night
I ask her to stroll
along the promenade
between the sloped pines.

In the paper that evening
I had read an article
that quoted
a famous anthropologist
about a recent unearthing.
3 $^1/_2$ million years ago
in a land we now call
Tanzania
two hominids walked
75 ft. and beyond
over a fresh layer of
volcanic ash
leaving footprints men
follow studiously
toward the faint light.

One was smaller
than the other, and probably
female. It was easy
to see
that she stopped, paused,
and turned to the left

to glance
at some possible threat
or irregularity,
and then continued to the north . . .

We stop
and glance off in the
same direction,
seeing nothing but
the faded moon abandoned
in the deep blue
of millions of skies, all that
time to
think over, and yet
we turn, a moment
of doubt,
inheriting the grace of hesitancy,
and then continue,
companions,
toward the faint
mysterious light . . .

IV

Brains linked to terminals
along an entire wall of computer,
a man and a woman
sit across from each other,
speechless,
hands at their sides,
alpha rays at full frequency,
no longer frustrated by
statements of love,
no longer spending lifetimes
with the strange lyricism of
the phrase *let me try to explain* . . .

In another time, call it ours,
my arms hold only
the small tremble of your desire.
It is so light, output a mere hundredth
of input, inadequacy giving way
to a fuller range
of grief,
but even that won't do.
Each time I kiss you
there are thousands of kisses . . .

How long
we tried to contain ourselves,
identity based on restraint,

unable to understand
the formula and potential for
the convective transmissions of energy,
the voltage ratio of three little words,

or, as the poet remarked,
the message inward converted
into the message out . . .

And so we strain under
the quirks of romance, still stunned
by the sudden glaze of infinity
in our eyes,
mute in our desire to shout back
the joy lodged in our throats,
routinely completing those
menial chores we come to
know as salvation.

Plugged into
a wall of computer
a man and a woman sit
speechless,
blind, each terrifying rush
an explosion of self
until they expand with the universe
at the fiery core of the brain.

And what are we
who can imagine these things,

scientists of a new order:
instrument or message?
wave or particle?

Creator? Archetype?

Variation? Flukes?

PART THREE

I

Here, Joseph,
in the far northern woods
away from everyone,
scanning the night sky
for the fixed pole star
of our earliest consciousness;
here,
tending the fire we lit
with a single match,
listening to the strange and sensible cries
of animals,
we place our hands forward
against the warmth,
unafraid, adjusting
to the silence and thought that grows
between father and son.

You huddle against me.
Even one of the few songs we know
would be dishonest.
Speech is a disguise; shelter a retreat.
Tonight, together,
the world is ours to make sense of.
Is it word or tool
that's made us what we are?
When the dust settles
and the ruins emerge, is it

the lizard's stare, that vast, patient honesty,
that keeps us hoping?

Son, once more
I divide my love.
How many times a man must,
or can,
I don't know.

Long ago
in the center
of the book of love
were the implicit, affectionate
instructions for
carrying on the species.
Between those pages we
pressed leaves
as if to preserve the simple design
of the instrument
most immediate

in our cyclical affair with the earth.
There too we divided our love,
knowing the earth
would make us whole.

For now there are
no certainties, many dreams.
Once more, son, I divide my love.

The Reptilian Interludes

This time
it's a woman with whom I've agreed on
a strange marital understanding:
no promises, no plans;
no project that requires
the strength or wit of two,
no children;
just a woman, merely man,
companionship our only bond.

Last year
it was an idea.
Before that the delicate balance
of a camshaft
and the obsession with speed.
Long ago
it was the uneven exchange of goods;
before that the power of my fist.
Once more, son,
I divide my love;
it is my way of understanding.
Fear is accumulative,
hope is a clever series of postponements,
but love is the dividing factor.

We zip up our sleeping bags.
This time your eyes close.
Mine remain open.
With your fingers you touch

the tiny hole in your mother's chest ...
Even the smallest opening is endless;
our memories are older than we are.
At the core of the star above
lies an ordinary stone;
or
at the center of this stone
the first, dazzling, petrified tear
of a star.

We must divide ourselves
to know for sure.
At the center of these woods
there's us, only us.
I don't know where we are;
the compass spins wildly
until I hold it
next to my heart.

There may be no future
to prepare for,
or no preparation for the future.
But each day
we seek the ageless nestle
of our own,
until we are glad
to the brink of tear.

The fact is, as in fiction,
a man

imagines his absence
the way a woman conceives
a multiple of presence.

Sleep, Joseph;
wake, place your lips and kiss;
we must believe in simplicity.
Sleep well, Joseph;
tomorrow we must gather wood,
swim
and find our way.
All over again, for the sake of our own,
we must find our way.

II

Again
in the corridors
I hear the screams and again
I arrive,
half-mad, in time
to grab the bloodied skull
from the sucking womb.
My fingers take hold of eye sockets
and nostrils
as I try to pull the child
from the dark vacuum
of a raging woman.

I put my mouth
on the burning cervix and bite
deep into the flesh.
The murky, swirling, microbial waters
spurt like haunted tears
into my eyes
and from within I hear
the stormy music of eumitosis
and blastula,
the fierce and soothing parturient winds
drawing back
its impossible promise;
until finally,
feeling myself drawn

to the black depth of a final,
continual reincarnation,
I make a vow to
sacrifice myself, call forth
God's name utterly in vain,
and in one last effort
yank the child free
and hold him out
in the suffocating daylight.
Exhausted, believing in the logic
of simple force,
I listen once more to the earth evolving
to the tidal weeping of man . . .

Suppose the universe were closed.

My son spends half the afternoon
trying to understand
the concept of zero energy,
how the universe
might be a flicker
in the vacuum of
some greater emptiness . . .

And I'm no help.

All I can tell you, son,
is that there are violent events
in the universe,

and between the equal quantities
of matter and anti-matter
we tiptoe like burglars sleepwalking
through their own cluttered homes.

I pick up the dusty, cracked
leather glove,
and the split bat

and tighten my hands around it
until my knuckles whiten

sending an old strength
through my arms and shoulders
and I swing, awkwardly
but with love
at the empty air.

Your face is lit
under the lamp on your desk
and your delicate flesh
has a pink glow.
Your long, elegant fingers
hold the page aloft, steady,
as if in that moment
of memorization
the simple fact of your being,
that casual grace,
becomes the only pure lesson
we ever learn.

Picking a book at random
off the shelf
I discover, inserted in the pages,
a torn set of instructions
for digging a well;
in my own handwriting there are
a few notes.
I've forgotten how many feet down
a man must go
into the earth.
I can't even tell you that, son,
But it is only a short way,
and unless the water table changes,
the water should flow
forever.

III

According to some popular
theory of performance
we reach a level of competency
and learn
how to advance ourselves
through others.

Then there's another
which suggests
we simply reminisce
until we lose sight
of what stirred us so
initially.

And then again
there's the psychic
who's so sick
of fucking up the dates of
minor catastrophes
he makes a fine art
out of observation and logic,
telling me, exactly,
the contents of my pockets . . .

But he did not guess
the two gold rings
upon which I etched, with a

piece of ordinary glass,
a few primitive scratches.
It is a small, summer wedding
we plan,
a backyard reception under
a lull of stars,
under the branches of the small hard
inedible fruit swelling
in the dark passage of ceremony,

which we wrote, together,
knowing full well
the music of our awkward vows
would fade more quickly
than the music which once swelled
under the chandelier
in the huge ballroom
where the last drunk couple
hung onto each other,
dragging their feet across the floor
in the hundred year marathon
for the spiritually crippled . . .

Still, the artifact precedes the meaning.
I polish the gold rings
and place them in a silk box.

The borrowed lace
would not hold the first symptoms

of our grief.
The something blue is
always a reflection, the sky the oceans,
ourselves our lives; always a faded blue.

And something old . . .
Our memories,
older than we are, to hold
something dearly
and not let go; the shoulder
of all our leanings,
a dial on a crystal radio
where each voice fades into static plea;
we hold on . . .
In our ridiculous fist
a small coin
which allows us to roam
however
briefly
through the hundred museums of
a beggar's palm . . .

The Reptilian Interludes

IV

My ambition fails me
like a pointless tradition.

Once
I tried to
make my way back, tried to
nap in the deathbed
where our fathers sang,
looked for the flag
and the stone courthouse it
flew over, and even in their absence
I searched
for the original birth certificate
buried deep now
in the vault of solitude.

Nor could I find
the small opening
where the water trickled forth,
the hidden stream
where a man sipped, rinsed the blood
from his hands
and followed his golden urine
back to the lost
oceanic treasures . . .

I am nothing more than
what I am,

learning finally
to see the world, after all, as it is.
With these hands,
which I hold before myself
like two pages of history,
I will bury the seed
and let hunger
take its dark root;
I will build a house of wood.
With the silk of a woman's hair
I will make my bed.

My glance skyward, whatever motive,
is nothing more
than a feather falling
through the billowing decades
of late afternoon.
Under the pillows of angels
who grew old
in the hypnotic mirrors of men
the gold tooth gleams,
single remaining artifact
sinking toward the hollow core, that peaceful
center toward which we drift
along with our effort
in a fading dream . . .

I take another shovelful of earth,
preparing the foundation

for the place I shall live.
I've forgotten how many feet down
a man must go.
It is a small wedding we plan,
and a small, spare room
for the childless hobbies of poetry
and physics.
According to some popular theory
we are nothing more
than what we are; gold is the substance
of rings and teeth;
and the water should flow forever.

PART FOUR

I

Tired, bored, myself, I flick on
the tape recorder
which lay on the nightstand
next to my son's bed.

All day,
at the sight of the new house,
ten wooded acres
fronting an unnamed river,
all day I've
cut, leveled and nailed
until the beams and joints took hold
like slowly spoken syllables
of a word suddenly understood:
Consolation

I am careful with a hammer,
alert to the excuses
of the nail-torn flesh and the
useless, recuperating dream.
My carpentry is basic,
no skylight in my blueprints.
In the final stages, I will oil
and wax the wood
not to see myself in the rich
deepening grain, the way men stare
into the polished counters of all night bars,

but to keep the wood from splitting
and releasing
that first irresistible warmth
of the perfumed sun . . .

On the recorder
I listen to a voice so clear,
my son's voice and yet not his,
reciting prayers
for the upcoming rite of communion.

Through me, oh Light of the Disembodied,
forbidden voices rise. Forgive me, I am
the dark, the sinner's soul that covets
men's eyes until, in the bewildering night,
they try to equate hope with fulfillment,
purpose with mortal love. There is no
darkness, only this secret altar of earthly
pride, upon which the knees fall, bleeding
openly, twin rivers of joy and despair.

In the name of the Father, who drifts over
us, elusive, sacramental, in an alpha high
of wind, wave, and of the Son, buried child
spreading the eternal root of amplitude and
frequency, and in the name of the holy Ghost,
fertilized and translucent in the starry crib
of the universe, I make my way, inefficient
conductor of Thy Light, confessor of old and

sentimental plots, over the dark gravel of
roads, this daily life.

Forgive me; I have fallen prey in the name
of love to the nostalgia of art, the false
leisure of science. May I rise, oh Light,
oh Light of the Disembodied, my fragmented
self the glowing pieces of your increate puzzle.
May the saints of the past, armed with their
holy formulas for measuring Light against the
blind containment of the eye, may those saints
shiver in the cold reason of spirit and stand
like exhausted scientists under the glory of Light . . .

All night we
sit before each other, hardly saying
a word, forgiving ourselves
the few incidental utterings
between us, knowing there is neither
speech nor language
to express the knowledge woven
into the dark yarn of your fingers;

What are you making?

In my lap
I hold a book I've been reading
all my life.
Why can't I turn the page?

Earlier, I tried to write
something poetic
for the upcoming ceremony . . . Instead
I drifted off
as I do now
to the last details of construction:
squaring the windows, hanging
the doors, attaching
the shingles. I know the chimney,
each brick a small volume of earth,
will be difficult, but the fire, there,
in the first chilly echo of inhabitance
will be easy, a match
held steady under dead wood, and the smoke
rising from the chimney
like the last faint notes
of an ancient civilization . . .

I look at you.
Your silence is a vow.
When the room begins to darken
your fingers move quickly
through the yarn, as if
you are darkness.

What is it you are making?
This page, why can't I turn it?

In another room
my son is doing an experiment,

attaching electrodes
to an animal's disembodied heart.
Later, when he speaks
into the recorder, the soft
beat of the heart
will fall like stresses over the words
of the prayer he is memorizing.

II

In the river, which seems
simpler than ever,
where gills and lungs reverse themselves
continually, in an evolutionary bow
to the whim of seasons and the
temperaments of suns;

in the river
that passes before the house nearly finished
where the rust of discarded containers
and the gold of buried lightning
flow together
under the quaint, reflective flicker
of some unimaginable solar storm,
my reflection quivers;

in the river
I place my pole, then
my hand,
then
my voice.
I do not lose myself, as the poet
claimed
and eventually pleaded,
the water filling his throat.

I am what I am,
lifting my head from the water,

my imagination
a preoccupying allegiance to
the dark of the closed lid,
the eye still rising
from dream to dream ...

In Rochester, New York
a young nun
prays in the dark corner of a room,
asking for forgiveness
not for herself, but for
the dead infant, just hours old,
that she pulled with almighty regret
from her own womb
and now lay stuffed in a bag
and wedged behind a dresser ...

It is the year 2000.

*When the personal ritual fails
the ceremony is doomed ...*

Ten miles outside
a small village is South America
900 believers in something
swallow the lump lodged in
their throats, that incomprehensible silence,
and chase it down with a
shot of cyanide,

and before them, his arms outstretched
as if orchestrating some final
lullaby of failure,
a man begins to collapse,
his vision rising from him like a dry wind
that blows the foul odor of the decomposed
over the swollen sea.

It is not a dream.
It is the year 2000.

When the personal ritual fails
The ceremony is doomed . . .

And there
on the peaceful edge
of some last prayer, some eternal riddle,
some unforgettable nursery rhyme,

A man talks to himself,
each word falling from the wall like plaster
until the house and the rubble are one
and the cold planet radiates
from within, bones
finally turning to light,
and drama finally frees itself from
the flaw of its making . . .

There,
where everything a man

has kept to himself becomes
his forever,
a reptile suns itself, balanced perfectly
upon an abandoned telescope.

. . . I plead not guilty, the 5th,
for my life.
Upon every doorknob, between every
exit, every entrance,
I leave this evidence, my future
in the warm print of my palm.

And in the warm parallel current
there in the swallow
of memory's river, how many
stupid, law-abiding men
are dragging up innumerable bodies . . .
Is this the evidence
sought by the prosecutor
in his unending campaign to prove
that decent men have died
embracing their reflections in the immeasurable depths
of man's oldest symbol . . .

I do not know;
I plead not guilty.
I sip the water, resolving the crises.

And later
I simply wipe the brass knob clean

until it gleams
like the skull of a cybernaut,
and walk off leaving no evidence,
considering no motive,
each step a denial of grace; the urge
to fly, the good sense to walk away.

III

I pick up the recorder
often now,
as if my son's prayers
were my own salvaged lullaby.
It is a communion
between body and knowledge
outside of ourselves, a prayer of
dread and desire, a song
at the far end of being.

I'm losing him.
That's the sad promise of the immortal,
two hands slipping out of
each other's grasp
and held out, like those of a beggar,
waiting for a bolt of fortune's light
to fill the palm . . .

Oh Disembodied One, there is but one sign
by which I shall be known in judgment,
dispersed like particles into the thunderous
clouds of heaven and surrounded by the
blinding Light of Glory, in which all hidden
things will lie revealed. Never before has
the intolerable sense of this unworthiness
pressed so heavily upon me; and yet Belief
grants me strength—whatever is broken within me

will be healed, whatever is unclean will be made
again pure.

The sign, in this humble state, can be read
in the Apocalypse that I bear on my face
like the seal of devotion as I stare into you.
This sign, oh Light, is my indulgence, the pain
I have endured in creating the fleeing concepts
through which I begin to understand a deeper need:
forgive the love that has bound me, the kindness
that has served as a reservoir of calm; forgive the
affection between us, that peaceful rebellion
against the divinity of the greater evolution;
forgive forgiveness, and the temptation to celebrate
what we have been.

So now I ponder, within this ancient heart, on
the limitless power that lies within You; and when
I consider the vastness of Your creation and peer
with these primitive eyes into the endless vistas
of space; when I recollect that behind all that is,
behind all that has been, You are; when I reflect
that for eons of years Your Spirit has hovered
unsearchably over destiny of men; then do I ask
for the radiant voices of angelic choirs, the mind
reeling before the unfathomed mystery; then do I ask
how my nothingness can be regarded as I subdue
my will, my heart, my reason, and in my transmission
to You, in this disembodiment of faith, I tear
from myself the veils of vain pretense . . .

With half-closed eyes
I see my finger
press the button on the recorder,
another last manual switch,
and doze off
toward another dream:
This time I've returned
to a country of abandoned structures
standing amidst the grey dust
that hangs in the silence
like a curtain in a condemned theatre.

At one time I would have
sung, yelled,
become dizzy with myself, slow-witted
and happy, out of step
but dancing
in the shadows of gods in the rafters,
a bit too proud and snubbing my nose
at the obvious,
crazed by performance,
a fool and a hero . . .

And this time,
be it stage or dream, love or pity,
eyes open, eyes closed,
I'd do it again, all over, audience be damned,
reeling under my own voice
until there in the sudden

light of a grand finale, myself a
mere shepherd,
I would place the child
deep in my arms, disobeying orders
and running off with him,
providing the infant
with at least a lifetime to prepare
for the news
someday we must sadly bear . . .

On a highway to Barstow
someone contemplates a neon lizard
smiling in the dark,
and even though its tail is busted
and won't wiggle anymore
the mouth still glows
and makes of Zeke's Café,
an establishment of the California desert,
a reference point for truckers
and other miserable souls
who haul back and forth in the lost sleep
that is theirs by right . . .

Someone else pours
one flask of vinegar into
another of piss, and waits for the oxidation,
the boil, the bubbling, whatever change a man inspires
in his quest for spontaneous perception.

Instead a
sweet odor rises
and the cats purr and brush up
against his leg
and he thinks about
swallowing the cheap concoction
and letting his heart drift
over the exotic wisps of this dark
unexpected potion . . .

Dear God,
forgive these experiments,
this hankering for the perfect fuel;
forgive the conjecture,
the hundred sensuous images
for a single passion.
I ask only
for one handsome flame
far down the corridor of the cracked mirror . . .

We arrive late in the afternoon
by boat
along the graceful bend
of this nameless river, the new house
finished, deep in a wooded setting
less than 50 yards away.

I point to the window
where I left the light burning.

Left behind for now, all
my regret, and in its place
the moderate sanctuary, a roof
that will not leak,
a door that opens into a measurable space.
My son and I step out
onto the shore,

But she just sits there
under a leafy scattering of light,
one hand touching the water
like the first ripple of a warmer current,
her head slightly raised
staring off
toward the vanishing point
that dissolves like mist in that unending merger
between earth and sky, distance
and abandon.

She is a portrait,
lovely in pose, fragile in posture;
time surrounds her
like a capsule of pure existence
and we leave her, lovingly,
rocking gently in a wooded boat
on the glimmering surface of the river.

And a few feet away
my son stops
and gazes straight into the
burning sun, his eyes finally
transparent to light, unblinking,
his body immobile, as if
in some inner glow he had been freed
from my cares, my warnings.

Within us, how many
simple warfares, call it art
if you must, have kept us
from staring out at the peaceful drift
of energy ahead.
I call him, but he
does not hear me anymore, the syllables
of his name a last lyric of love
lost finally
to that faint echo still fading
in a huge gallery of unused air . . .

He is the future,
I acknowledge, shamefully, and
leave him there
on the shore, the transmission begun,
the veils of pretense torn away,
the light and the body one,
the first shadows of twilight
my singular possession.

So I turn to the house,
and begin walking toward it.
The frame is solid, and I resolve
not to look back;
but as I move toward the house
it begins receding.

For a moment
I close my eyes, as if to become
the dreamer again.
The strength of the beams pass through me
until my legs push harder
against the earth, and I begin running,
but the house recedes
at the same quickening pace.

Somewhere before an oscilloscope
a man stands hypnotized . . .

I run, and the house recedes,
and there is still another equation
I must learn
between fundamental need and withdrawal.
I try to clear my mind
of a million years,
and run, and watch the house
drifting away at every step
of my approach.
I think if only the light in the window

were not burning
the darkness would soothe me;

And when it is dark, as I know it will be,
my memory will be a single flame.

finis

COMMENTARY

Ross Talarico is one of our best and most important poets. *The Reptilian Interludes* is another landmark in a career by a poet and writer who has quietly but profoundly made a case for literature and writers having a role in our culture. Significantly, as this country's only full-time writer-in-residence for an entire city, he has enriched whole communities through his efforts—winning such honors as *The Mina P. Shaughnessy Prize, The Lillian Fairchild Award,* and being named *Langston Hughes Poet/Scholar.* In addition, he has reached beyond the academic settings which contain his art and has been featured as a genuine populist writer in such unlikely places as *The Today Show, National Public Radio's Weekend Edition,* and *USA Today.* Now, with this modern-day epic poem, he takes an even broader view, a look at the species itself as it evolves scientifically and devolves humanistically and calls to question the design between science and art in a nostalgic farewell to mankind as traditionally defined. Surely Talarico has considered his art and the issues surrounding it with a unique vision, a writer who has consistently stepped outside the mainstream assumptions of American Letters, challenging the status quo and fascinating those readers who require that deepening sense of purpose in a world that both evolves and devolves often under the tutelage of a single interior voice.

As a writer of poetry, novels, personal essays, and more, Talarico has never backed away from addressing the kinds of difficult questions for which there are no easy answers. And like other ambitious poets wrestling with the purpose of human existence on grand scales—think of Dante or Milton—Talarico expresses his view through a specific and very familiar everyday world. Who are we? Why are we here? Where are we heading as a species? How are we to respond to that journey we call life? Dante often portrayed his mission of life's meaning through people he knew but who also served as universally recognized types. And what intimate relationship holds more universal significance than that of of Adam and Eve in Milton's *Paradise Lost*? Similarly, Talarico uses the death of a mother, the development of a son, his love for women and more to introduce his readers to new understandings of what it means to be human in a world where the god of Dante and Milton has been replaced by the god of science and technology.

In its length, structure and tone, *The Reptilian Interludes* resembles the two greatest and most well-known of all modernist poems: T. S. Eliot's "The Wasteland" and "The Love Song of J. Alfred Prufrock." As in "The Wasteland," the landscape of Talarico's poem is bleak and foreboding, but its language is not despairing. Neither are the personally intimate scenes that contrast with the impersonal climate created by technology. And like Prufrock, Talarico's narrator is in the autumn years of his life and taking a long, hard look at what he's harvested. The poem opens with his heading home to bed, but his stopping at a store for a book of matches also marks his entry into a darker, interior world in which he hopes to shed some light. Accompanying the narrator into the heart of human darkness are his son Joseph and Talarico's readers. Fortunately, we're in good hands.

Since he was a child, the narrator has had an attraction to and fascination with tools. He can repair a car; he can even build a small house. But the tools of his youth—objects he could control—have been overrun by a technology that is almost beyond imagination. It includes everything from electrodes planted in babies' brains to the mounting of guns on people's eyes so other people can be killed with an effort that is no greater that the lifting of an eyebrow. And just as quickly. In such a world, the narrator—like his tools, and like Talarico the poet himself—has become obsolete. The anti-poems of science and technology are like runaway trains that have left a station with self-reflection, appreciation of nature, confidence in intention, and the expression of values traditionally associated with what used to be called "truth" standing on the platform. And the tools for living that the narrator has acquired and wants to pass on to his son are as irrelevant as he is. Showing Joey how to toss a baseball or light a campfire with just one match are as much use to him as a hammer in a science lab.

But Talarico isn't recommending a return to traditional humanistic values. He knows they're history, and it's just a matter of time before he and like-minded poets are just as well. Instead, Talarico creates an interlude between the human evolution of the past and the devolution of the present, a breathing space in which we can contemplate his proposal for a new, energy-transforming definition of what it means to be human. The journey toward this definition is not an easy one, but it is one that is worthy of our intention, consideration, and for those willing to take the risk, action.

—RICHARD ANDERSEN, Rome, March 2007

Ross Talarico has published hundreds of poems, in such places as *The North American Review, The Atlantic Monthly, Poetry, The American Poetry Review, Prairie Schooner, The Nation, The Iowa Review, Shenandoah, Poetry Northwest, The Southern Poetry Review,* and *The Southern California Anthology.* His awards and honors range from the prestigious *Mina P. Shaughnessy Prize* and the *Lillian Fairchild Award,* to NBCs *Sportsman of the Week, The Langston Hughes Poet/Scholar* designation from the University of Kansas, and a New York State Department of Recreation Program of the Year Award. His poetic narratives from oral histories of others in his book *Hearts and Times: The Literature of Memory,* were adapted for the stage in Chicago, and his popular human interest columns appeared for several years in Gannett newspapers. He has been a keynote or featured speaker at several major literary, educational and popular culture conferences. He lives with his four children in Southern California where he is Professor of Writing and Literature at Springfield College's San Diego campus. Talarico is a multi-genre author with several books, and he has just completed his new and selected poems, and a novel about race relations based on a fictional account of the true crime of America's only convicted Black serial killer.

Richard Andersen is a former Fulbright professor, James Thurber Writer-in-Residence, and Karolyi Foundation Fellow. His books include novels, critical studies, and books on writing.

Frederick Turner, Professor of Arts and Humanities at the University of Texas at Dallas, was educated at Oxford University. A poet, critic, translator, philosopher, and former editor of *The Kenyon Review,* he has authored 27 books, including *The Culture of Hope, Genesis, Hadean Ecologues, Shakespeare's Twenty First Century Economics, Paradise, The Prayers of Dallas,* and *Natural Religion.*

VIA FOLIOS

*A refereed book series dedicated to Italian studies
and the culture of Italian Americans in North America*

RACHEL GUIDO DE VRIES
Teeny Tiny Tino's Fishing Story
Vol. 47, Childrens' Literature, $6

EMANUEL DI PASQUALE
Writing Anew
Vol. 46, Poetry, $15

MARIA FAMÀ
Looking For Cover
Vol. 45, Poetry, $12

ANTHONY VALERIO
*Toni Cade Bambara's
One Sicilian Night*
Vol. 44, Poetry, $10

EMANUEL CARNEVALI
Dennis Barone, Ed.
Furnished Rooms
Vol. 43, Poetry, $14

BRENT ADKINS, et. al., Eds.
Shifting Borders, Negotiating Places
Vol. 42, Proceedings, $18

GEORGE GUIDA
Low Italian
Vol. 41, Poetry, $11

GARDAPHÉ, GIORDANO,
& TAMBURRI
Introducing Italian Americana
Vol. 40, ItalAmerStudies, $10

DANIELA GIOSEFFI
*Blood Autumn /
Autunno di sangue*
Vol. 39, Poetry, $15 / $25

FRED MISURELLA
Lies to Live by
Vol. 38, Stories, $15

STEVEN BELLUSCIO
Constructing a Bibliography
Vol. 37, Ital.Americana, $15

ANTHONY J. TAMBURRI, Ed.
Italian Cultural Studies 2002
Vol. 36, Essays, $18

BEA TUSIANI
con amore
Vol. 35, Memoir, $19

FLAVIA BRIZIO-SKOV, Ed.
*Reconstructing Societies
in the Aftermath of War*
Vol. 34, History, $30

TAMBURRI, et. al., Eds.
Italian Cultural Studies 2001
Vol. 33, Essays, $18

ELIZABETH G. MESSINA, Ed.
In Our Own Voices
Vol. 32, ItalAmerStudies, $25

STANISLAO G. PUGLIESE
Desperate Inscriptions
Vol. 31, History, $12

HOSTERT & TAMBURRI, Eds.
Screening Ethnicity
Vol. 30, ItalAmerCulture, $25

G. PARATI & B. LAWTON, Eds.
Italian Cultural Studies
Vol. 29, Essays, $18

HELEN BAROLINI
More Italian Hours
Vol. 28, Fiction, $16

FRANCO NASI, Ed.
Intorno alla Via Emilia
Vol. 27, Culture, $16

ARTHUR L. CLEMENTS
The Book of Madness & Love
Vol. 26, Poetry, $10

JOHN CASEY, et. al.
Imagining Humanity
Vol. 25, InterdiscStudies, $18

Published by Bordighera, Inc., an independently owned not-for-profit scholarly organization that has no legal affiliation to the
University of Florida, the John D. Calandra Italian American Institute, or State University of New York at Stony Brook.

Book design by Lisa Cicchetti

www.ingramcontent.com/pod-product-compliance
Lightning Source LLC
Chambersburg PA
CBHW020905090426
42736CB00008B/504